1 Magic Rabbit

Pizza   Jar

Snake   Tie

Button   Bell

Lollipop

Golf Club

Hidden Pictures
1-2-3 PUZZLES

HIGHLIGHTS PRESS

Honesdale, Pennsylvania

2 Playful Kids

Ruler

Frog

Cookie

Teacup

Horseshoe

Comb

Moon

Umbrella

3

Umbrella   Watch

Mitten   Boot

Pizza   Crown

Bread   Button

Belt

4

4 Yummy Waffles

Canoe

Sock

Butterfly

Crayon

Fish

Skateboard

Musical Note

5 Busy Critters

Lollipop

Sock

Mug

Horseshoe

Pencil

Straw

Shovel

Baseball

Baseball Cap

6 Baseball Caps

Boot

Glove

Key

Golf Club

Umbrella

Snail

Hammer

Horseshoe

Ruler

Button

Belt

Pizza

Domino

Kite

Moon

Golf Club

Lollipop

Magnet

8 Paper Airplanes

8

Coin

Tire

Bell

Hourglass

Heart

Watch

Horseshoe

Worm

Paintbrush

Bread

9

Sock

Pie

Tie

Guitar

Potato

Handbag

Tomato

Star

10 Wiggly Worms

Toothbrush

Crayon

Button

Mitten

Magnifying Glass

Lollipop

Ruler

Flute

11

Snail

Boomerang

Boot

Egg

Book

Pennant

Megaphone

Teacup

Lemon

Jump Rope

12 Perfect Pizzas

12

Hockey Stick

Fish

Comb

Toothbrush

Straw

Sock

Canoe

Baseball

Pennant

Yo-Yo

13

Dress

Crown

Magnifying Glass

Teacup

Ice-pop

Dog

Pennant

Pickle

14 Crazy Clowns

Mitten

Carrot

Flag

Acorn

Ruler

Envelope

Book

Spoon

Toothbrush

Snake

15

15 Terrific Teddy Bears

Saw

Ruler

Watch

Football

Envelope

Carrot

Bowl

Horseshoe

Mushroom

16 Pretty Flowers

Screwdriver

Pizza

Umbrella

Spoon

Teacup

Crayon

Crown

Ruler

Toothbrush

17

Pencil

Moon

Pizza

Toothbrush

Envelope

Horseshoe

Belt

Stick of Gum

Hockey Stick

Crown

18 Friendly Fish

18

Spaceship

Straw

Bow

Moon

Teacup

Ring

Party Hat

Domino

Comb

Camera

19

Envelope

Lightning Bolt

Ladder

Pizza

Party Hat

Glove

Golf Club

Snake

Moon

Candy Cane

20 Bright Balloons

Lightning Bolt

Glove

Boomerang

Pizza

Baseball Cap

Magnet

Moon

Feather

Pennant

Crayon

Blast Off!
Can you count 20 stars?

1

2

3

4

5

6

7

8

9

10

Balloon

Flashlight

Belt

Feather

Envelope

Spatula

Wedge of Lime

Pencil   Suitcase   Button   Pizza   Eyeglasses   Ghost

Party Hat

Sock

Umbrella

Horseshoe

Crown

Ruler

Straw

11
12
13
14
15
16
17
18
19
20

23

ANSWERS

cover

page 2

page 3

page 4

page 5

page 6

page 7

page 8

page 9

page 10

page 11

page 12